I0621265

GOD, **WHATEVER** IT TAKES FOR REVIVAL TO LAST

FAITH THAT STANDS
WHEN HEADLINES FADE

Janet Little Cooper

God, Whatever It Takes For Revival To Last
Faith That Stands When Headlines Fade

All rights reserved. No part of this book may be reproduced, stored, or transmitted in any form or by any means without written permission from the author, except for brief quotations used in reviews or articles.

Published by: With My Father's Hands Publishing

Pensacola, Florida, USA

ISBN: 979-827-425-2003

Disclaimer: This book is nonfiction, reflecting the author's personal experiences and interpretations.

Scripture References: Unless noted otherwise, Scripture quotations are from the *New International Version (NIV)*, ©1973, 1978, 1984, 2011 by Biblica, Inc. Used with permission.

With My Father's Hands was founded to honor both the legacy of my earthly father and the eternal presence of my Heavenly Father. Through the handwritten sermons written by my father, Rev. Thomas Little, Jr., which he left to me when he died in 2016, his words continue to teach, encourage, and inspire.

Just as my father's hands once penned messages of truth and wisdom, and just as God's hands have guided me and sustained me in life and this book, this name represents a mission to carry forward that same calling of sharing words that uplift, strengthen, and bring light to those who read them.

Connect With Me

a www.amazon.com/author/Janet Little Cooper

✉ withmyfathershands@gmail.com

f Janet Little Cooper or Life According to Janet

◎ www.instagram.com/by-janetlittlecooper

♪ www.tiktok.com/@janet.cooper7

DEDICATION

Dedicated to my son, Austin.
You are a walking testament of God's mercy and faithfulness. Your life is
a constant reminder of God's love and that love endures all things

* * *

In memory of my son, Bryant.
How I miss you, but the memory of your contagious smile is always with me.
Your strength, faith, and unwavering love inspire me daily.
I will carry you in my heart until the day we are reunited.

TABLE OF CONTENTS

A Dangerous Prayer

Some prayers are safe.

We ask for God's blessing, protection, and guidance. These prayers are good, comfortable, and inexpensive.

But then there are the prayers that shake the heavens and demand surrender— prayers that come not from a place of comfort, but from desperation.

That is where I found myself as a mother standing in a high school locker room. Surrounded by football helmets and shoulder pads, the smell of sweat and turf in the air, I whispered words that would change my life:

"God, whatever it takes to bring Austin back to You."

I didn't know what those words would require.
I didn't know that within weeks my son's femur would snap in two on the practice field, or that I would hear doctors whisper "bone cancer" in sterile hospital halls. I didn't know the nights I would spend in the NICU watching monitors flicker and praying for another heartbeat, another breath.

All I knew in that moment was this: my son had drifted from the God he once professed, and I loved him too much to settle for anything less than his whole heart returning to Christ.

What I prayed that day was dangerous because it demanded surrender. It meant letting go of my plans, comfort, and even my expectations as a mother. It meant entrusting Austin's life—fully and without condition—into God's hands.

And God answered, not in the way I imagined, but in a way that revealed His power, faithfulness, and call to revival. This book was born from that prayer.

It is about what happens when we dare to ask God for revival. It is about the cost of that revival, the miracles that sustain it, and the lessons learned when bitterness threatens to choke it out.

It is also about something bigger than my family's story. Revival has always been costly. From the blood of the martyrs in scripture to the lives of bold men and women today—even in the wake of Charlie Kirk's assassination in 2025—God has shown that what the enemy intends for evil, He uses for good.

So as you turn these pages, I invite you into that dangerous prayer. To whisper it for yourself, your children, your church, your nation. To trust that the God who hears is also the God who redeems. Because a revival that lasts always begins with a prayer that costs us everything.

Chapter 1

THE PRAYER OVER THE LOCKER

"God, whatever it takes to get Austin's attention."

The smell of sweat and turf lingered in the air as I entered the football locker room. Rows of metal doors lined the walls, each marked with the name and number of a boy chasing Friday night lights. Our church had gathered the evening before the annual See You at The Pole student-led prayer event to walk the high school campus, praying over classrooms, teachers, and students.

Another mother and I stepped into the football locker room, where that season's hopes and struggles seemed to hang thick in the air.

I stopped in front of one locker—my son Austin's. The space held more than pads and cleats. It held pieces of his heart. I laid my hand on the cool metal, bowed my head, and whispered a prayer that came from the deepest part of me:

"God, whatever it takes to get Austin's attention… whatever it takes to draw him back to You, do it. Help him love You more than he loves football. I surrender him to Your will."

It was the hardest and most freeing prayer I had ever prayed. Every mother's instinct is to protect her child from harm, yet here I was telling God to do whatever it took—even if that meant pain, loss, or heartbreak. My voice trembled, but my heart knew it was right. Austin belonged to God before he ever belonged to me.

The other mom snapped a picture, capturing a scene I didn't realize would mark the beginning of a journey. At the time, it was just a prayer walk. But heaven was listening. Within weeks, I would understand the weight of my words.

Austin had given his life to Christ as a little boy at Vacation Bible School, when his blue eyes sparkled and his chubby cheeks flushed with excitement over life. My father—his "Papa"—baptized him not long after, a moment that felt like the passing of a spiritual torch. But as high school crept in, so did distance. Football, friends, and the swirl of teenage life seemed to crowd out the simple faith of his childhood.

As his mother, I could see it. His heart wasn't fully set on God, and that reality burdened me in ways only a praying parent can understand.

So that day at his locker, my prayer wasn't casual—it was desperate. It was surrender. It asked God to write Austin's story in a way that brought him back close, no matter the cost.

I didn't know then how quickly that prayer would be tested.
At Austin's locker, I had released my grip and handed him fully to God… and before long, I would learn what that meant.

Chapter 2

THE TEST BEGINS

It was a nightmare unfolding in slow motion

Two weeks after my prayer at Austin's locker, the call came from football practice. The voice on the other end—his trainer—sounded calm: "Austin is hurt, but it's just his knee. You need to pick him up."

But when I arrived, it was clear this was no ordinary injury.When I saw his distorted leg, I knew immediately it wasn't his knee—it was something far worse.

We didn't know it then but my son's femur had completely snapped in two. The swelling, the agony, and the hurried way he was moved—from the ground to a golf cart, to a picnic table, and into the backseat of my car—felt like a nightmare unfolding in slow motion.

Later, I learned his injury should have been treated as a medical emergency requiring urgent transport. A month earlier, an MRI ordered for a swollen knee had appeared normal to his provider, so she assumed the new injury was simply a recurrence of the same issue. That assumption influenced ever rushed decision that followed.

The orthopedic surgeon told me to bring Austin to her office. In hindsight, I should have gone with my motherly instinct and demanded he be transferred to a hospital. The X-ray at the orthopedist's office confirmed what my heart already knew. I dropped to my knees when I saw the image of my son's bone. His leg was broken clean apart, the bone shifted dangerously side by side. In that moment, fear screamed louder than faith.

Yet, even there, God was present. A police officer overheard the chaos and Austin's cries at the orthopedics' office, where his son was waiting to be seen. He stepped out of his son's room to see what was happening, saw the X-ray, and immediately called 911 on his radio.. Within minutes, paramedics arrived, furious that Austin was referred to the doctor's office instead of a hospital emergency room. Paramedics quickly administered morphine, stabilized him, and rushed him to the children's hospital. By this time, Austin had endured extreme pain for three hours.

Austin's life should have ended on that field

By every human measure, Austin's life should have ended on that field, the golf cart, the picnic table, or in the backseat of my car. His femoral artery could have been severed at any moment. But it wasn't.

And that's when the truth of Romans 8:28 was the apparent reality of our lives: "And we know that in all things God works for the good of those who love him, who have been called according to his purpose."

Even through the mistakes, oversights, and negligence, God was weaving protection over my boy.

Miracle #1: God spared Austin's life despite human error after human error.

In the film taken at the doctor's office, the same orthopedic surgeon who had released him just a month earlier finally admitted what she had missed before: a stress fracture in his femur. It had been there all along, overlooked in the MRI she had declared "clear". That missed fracture was the very reason his bone had snapped in two.

Once at the hospital, the Chief Orthopedic Surgeon didn't even review those X-rays or read the notes from Austin's doctor. Instead, he took more X-rays and with clinical certainty, he told me he suspected bone cancer. "The femur of a healthy fifteen-year-old boy doesn't just snap in two," he said flatly.

His words shattered me. That fear—bone cancer—should never have been spoken. But it was, and it held us hostage for days while test after test was run to rule it out. Austin remained in excruciating pain, waiting, while I tried to breathe under the crushing weight of those words.

> ## What the enemy meant for destruction, God was already working to redeem

In those sleepless nights, I clung to Jesus' promise: "In this world you will have trouble. But take heart! I have overcome the world" (John 16:33).

I repeated it like a lifeline. Looking back, I see those days differently. That spoken fear—the very shadow whispered over Austin—would become reality years later in my youngest son, Bryant. His cancer diagnosis and passing would one day confirm the very fear spoken prematurely over his brother.

The trouble was real, but so was the One who promised victory. And as I sat by Austin's hospital bed, Joseph's words to his brothers in Genesis 50:20 felt like they belonged to me and Austin too: "You intended to harm me, but God intended it for good."

What the enemy meant for destruction, God was already working to redeem.

Chapter 3

IN THE VALLEY OF DECISION

Austin's oxygen dropped.
Alarms blared. Nurses rushed in.

At the children's hospital in Pensacola, I thought the worst was behind us. After the brutal days of scans to rule out bone cancer, Austin's femur was finally set, surgery complete, and maybe—just maybe—we could breathe again.

But that night, everything unraveled.

Austin's oxygen dropped. Alarms blared. Nurses rushed in. Tests revealed a blood clot in his lung. A piece had broken loose from the massive clot in his leg and traveled upward, threatening his life. Doctors warned us that more fragments could break free at any time.

The prognosis was grim. They began blood thinners, but instead of improving, Austin declined. Then came the impossible choice: a clot-buster procedure—his only hope, they said. But the risk was staggering: 50/50. Survive or die.

I was handed the papers to sign, trembling as I held the pen. How could a mother make that choice for her 15-year-old child? I couldn't without first asking the team of doctors to join hands with me and our pastor.

I told them I didn't know if they were Christians, but I believed God had gifted them with knowledge and skilled hands to operate and I was trusting them for that reason; but, I entrusted my son to God.

I stepped into the parking lot, grabbed my Bible out of my car, and called my parents. Through tears, I said, "Surely God won't take another child from our family. He just wouldn't."

My oldest brother's seven-year-old daughter, Reagan had died years earlier (in July, the seventh month of the year) from viral meningitis. The number seven seemed etched into our family's story as we witnessed it time and time again. What was seen as a number of completion in Scripture, the number seven marked incompleteness for me at the time.

On the other end, my mother's voice was steady: "Janet, the question isn't whether God heals Austin. The question is, if He decides to take Austin home, will you still love Him? Will you still serve Him? Will you still obey Him?"

Her words echoed those of Job: "Though he slay me, yet will I hope in him" (Job 13:15).

Almost immediately, the doctors returned. Their plan had changed. The clot-buster would not be performed. An out-of-town specialist warned Austin would not survive it.

Miracle #2: God stayed the doctors' hands.

As the days passed, James 1:2–4 became clearer: "Consider it pure joy, my brothers and sisters, whenever you face trials of many kinds, because you know that the testing of your faith produces perseverance.

The valley was deep, but God's hand was deeper.

Chapter 4

HELD IN HIS HANDS

God dissolved the clot and spared his life again

Austin remained in the NICU for fifteen days. Every day felt like both victory and defeat. He had to relearn walking-three steps, then five, then ten. Each number marked determination born of pain.

One day, weary from it all, tears streaming, he looked at me and said: "Mama, I'm going to be in church every service I can after this."

That vow took me back to my prayer at his locker: "God, whatever it takes to bring him back to You." It was happening.

Two days after release, Austin's leg swelled. An ultrasound suggested another clot. Though sent home with orders to begin physical therapy the following week, my spirit was unsettled. His pediatrician secured an appointment at a children's hospital in Alabama for a second opinion. There, doctors diagnosed an aneurysm instead of a clot. Physical therapy would have been deadly. Surgery was scheduled. Ten minutes after it began, the surgeon called me. My heart sank—until he said: "The aneurysm we saw is gone Every vein and artery is healthy. There's nothing there."

Miracle #3: God healed the aneurysm before doctors could.

Six months of blood thinners, needles, and monitoring followed. Pain and frustration were constant companions. Yet Austin was alive-walking proof of God's mercy. Three miracles. One boy. Countless prayers answered.

Hebrews 12:6 gave me perspective: "Because the Lord disciplines the one he loves, and he chastens everyone he accepts as his son."

Austin's suffering was not punishment but shaping—a father disciplining a son He loved. God had answered my desperate prayer, not in the way I imagined but in ways
that forever marked our family.

Chapter 5

WHERE I FELL SHORT

Instead of giving the hurt to God, I let bitterness take root

Austin's urgency to return to church was held for six months. Blood thinner shots, hospital visits, and monthly checkups consumed our days. His words from the PICU—"Mama, I'm going to be in church every service I can after this"—echoed in my mind constantly.

When the day of release finally came, I was eager. I wanted this to be a new beginning, a fresh fire, fulfilling the prayer I had whispered at his locker.

But what should have been a homecoming quickly turned sour.

Not once during Austin's hospital stay, his surgeries, or his grueling recovery had his youth minister called or visited. Not one prayer at his bedside. Not one word of encouragement for a boy who had faced death three times. Our pastor was there through it all.

The silence pierced me. I expected joy, but instead, I felt betrayal that morning in church when this same youth minister publicly welcomed an older adult who used a wheelchair back to church but remained silent when Austin returned for the first time. I spoke up to bring the attention I felt Austin deserved. Only then was he recognized.

Instead of laying that disappointment at Jesus' feet, I let it take root in me. My hurt turned into anger, which hardened into resentment. Slowly, that resentment poisoned my heart. I knew better. I grew up in church and in the home of a Southern Baptist preacher. Honestly, though, the anger wasn't all the result of one persons actions or lack there of. My heart was already in a fragile state of brokenness because I was newly divorced and deeply hurt.

Scripture warns us of this very danger:
"See to it that no one falls short of the grace of God and that no bitter root grows up to cause trouble and defile many." (Hebrews 12:15)

That's precisely what happened. I let bitterness take root, and it didn't just trouble me—it defiled the very revival God was birthing in our home.

At first, we still went through the motions. But the weight in my heart grew heavier with every service. My attendance faltered. My encouragement to my boys faltered. Before long, we stopped going altogether.

The revival I had prayed for at Austin's locker, sparked by his tearful vow in the NICU, was smothered— not by crisis, but by my bitterness.

Peter's words ring true in 1 Peter 4:12–13:
"Dear friends, do not be surprised at the fiery ordeal that has come on you to test you… But rejoice inasmuch as you participate in the sufferings of Christ."

I expected persecution or hardship to test us. But I never expected neglect and disappointment from within the church. Yet that too was a test. And in that season, I failed it.

Looking back, I can see the enemy's strategy clearly. If he couldn't take Austin's life through a broken femur, a blood clot, or an aneurysm, he would attack our hearts through bitterness.

And I let him.

That was my failure as Austin's mom.

The truth is, God had been faithful. He answered my desperate prayer, "God, whatever it takes." But instead of guarding the spark He lit in my son, I let offense choke it out. I focused on people's failures instead of God's faithfulness.

The downward spiral began there. And like every spiral, it didn't stop with me—it pulled my boys down too.

I had heard that prayer my entire life growing up—"Jesus, send revival." I thought revival meant a series of services, fiery preaching, and crowded altars. But revival is more than an event on a calendar. God is awakening His people, restoring their hearts, and drawing them back to Himself.

Revival is threatened by tragedy and tested by disappointment. The question is not only, "Can I trust God in the valley of sickness?" but also, "Can I trust Him when His people fail me?"

Even in my failures, God was still working. But the revival in our home would not last until I learned to root my faith deeper than people, deeper than feelings, deeper than disappointment.

Because only faith rooted in Christ alone can endure.

Chapter 6

When the Fire Fades

If anyone had reason to stand in gratitude, it was us

After Austin's release from the hospital, the urgency to serve God burned strongly in his heart. He had said it himself in the NICU. God had spared his life three times. If anyone had reason to stand in gratitude and devotion, it was us.

But our return to church was short-lived. My hurt turned into bitterness, and that bitterness became a barrier. Over time, the fire we had felt in those desperate hospital nights faded into a dull ember. Revival was delayed because I had allowed disappointment to take root.

And isn't that the way it so often happens? In the aftermath of a crisis, hearts turn toward God, but unless that spark is fed and guarded, it fades.

I saw it in my own home. But I've also seen it in our nation.

After the terrorist attacks on 9/11, America came together in a way I had never witnessed before. Churches were packed. Strangers prayed together in public. Flags flew from every porch and every car window. There was unity, humility, and even repentance. But within a few years, the crowds thinned. The flags disappeared. Patriotism and faith gave way once more to distraction, division, and complacency. Our country no longer stood in unity but slowly fell into a downward spiral of division and hatred.

It is that same spirit of division and hatred that ultimately surrounded the tragic killing of public speaker Charlie Kirk, whose bold, uncompromising faith made him a target in a nation increasingly hostile toward truth.

A spiritual awakening has begun

Yet even in his death, something remarkable happened. Vigils. Prayer gatherings. Voices lifted in unity. Community baptism services are being held all across America. People are talking openly about faith, about courage, about truth. Churches are filling with people who haven't stepped inside a sanctuary in years. Lost people are being saved. Lukewarm believers are being stirred awake. It has been a tremendous spiritual awakening—sparked by the boldness of one man's faith, lived publicly and unapologetically, even unto death.

We all want our lives to count like that. As Christians, we all want to leave behind a faith that awakens others. But the question still presses in on me: Will it last?

Because revival is not the same thing as a movement of emotion. Revival is not just packed churches, tears at an altar, or headlines filled with hope. Those things can be beautiful beginnings—but if they are not rooted in God's Word, nurtured through prayer, strengthened in community, and lived out in daily surrender, they will fade as quickly as they flared.

Jesus warned us in Luke 8:13 about shallow roots—that some "receive the word with joy when they hear it, but they have no root. They believe for a while, but in the time of testing they fall away."

That's the danger of revival born only out of crisis. If it doesn't grow roots, it withers when the emotions fade.

I saw it happen in my own home. The fire that burned in my whispered prayers at my son's locker was real and in Austin's hospital bed. But when disappointment came, I let bitterness smother it. The same danger threatens us now as a nation.

I think of Austin's struggle to take those first painful steps in the NICU. Each day, he grew stronger—not because of a single burst of determination, but because he kept showing up, one step at a time. That's how faith grows too. That's how revival lasts.

Hebrews 12:1–2 urges us to "throw off everything that hinders and the sin that so easily entangles… and run with perseverance the race marked out for us, fixing our eyes on Jesus."

Revival is not a sprint. It is a marathon of perseverance. And unless we root ourselves in Christ, our fire will flicker out just as quickly as it was lit.

So the question remains: What makes revival last?

Chapter 7

REVIVAL
THAT LAST

If revival is built only on passion,
it will fade when the headlines change

By the time Austin had survived three brushes with death, I felt certain revival in our home was inevitable. How could it not be? God had worked miracles before our very eyes. Austin had promised through tears in a hospital room that he would be in church every time the doors were open. That moment felt like spiritual victory sealed and delivered.

But I learned something the hard way: revival doesn't last simply because of an emotional moment, a promise made in a crisis, or even miraculous healing. Revival lasts only when it is nurtured, guarded, and rooted in Christ.

I used to think revival was something that happened at church—a special week of services or a moment of powerful worship that left me breathless. But true revival is far more personal. It begins deep inside a surrendered heart and grows outward like a steady flame. It is carried into hospital rooms, grocery store aisles, ball fields, and homes. It is not an event we attend—it is a life we live.

As I reflected on revival in our nation, I realized the same truth applied. America has seen passionate responses in moments of crisis—after 9/11, and again after the tragic loss of a bold Christian cultural leader whose public faith and uncompromising message challenged the nation. When he was killed in an act of violence, believers across the country were shaken.

Yet even in that darkness, something remarkable happened. Vigils formed. Prayer gatherings spread. Voices lifted in unity. Community baptisms took place across America. People began talking openly about faith, courage, and truth. Churches filled with people who hadn't stepped inside a sanctuary in years. The lost were saved. Lukewarm believers were stirred awake. It became a powerful spiritual awakening.

But if revival is built only on passion, it will fade when headlines change. Revival rooted only in emotion will waver when trials come.

I began to understand that revival is not sustained by feelings but by the firm foundation of God's Word. Emotions fade—but truth remains. Jesus told His disciples in Matthew 24:35, "Heaven and earth will pass away, but my words will never pass away." When I let resentment take root, it was because I had shifted my focus away from Scripture and onto people. I expected people to hold me up when only God's Word was meant to anchor me.

The prayer that began in a locker room—"God, whatever it takes to bring my son back to You"—initially felt like a moment of fire. But true revival continued only when I clung to God's Word every day that followed.

As I prayed more deeply, I began to see that revival is also sustained by prayer itself. The same God who heard my desperate whisper over a metal locker is the God who strengthened Austin through painful steps, hospital beds, and weary nights. Prayer was the lifeline that kept faith alive when my emotions faltered. Paul's instruction became my lifeline: "Pray without ceasing" (1 Thessalonians 5:17).

There were days when prayer was a whispered groan. Other days, it was bold declaration. But prayer kept my heart tethered to Christ.

Then, I remembered something simple but essential—revival grows stronger in community. During Austin's hospital stay, I gathered his doctors with our pastor to join hands in prayer. That circle reminded me of the early church in Acts 2:42: "They devoted themselves to the apostles' teaching and to fellowship, to the breaking of bread and to prayer." Revival flourished among them because they lived it together.

When I later pulled away from church out of pain and disappointment, I unintentionally pulled my family away from the very community God designed to help sustain us. Isolation suffocated revival, while fellowship had helped it thrive. I learned we cannot protect revival alone; we must walk with others—strengthening one another's flame.

As the months passed, God pressed another truth into my heart: revival lasts only when we surrender. The most dangerous prayer I ever prayed—"God, whatever it takes"—required surrender. And surrender is rarely comfortable. It cost me control, pride, and often my understanding.

Jesus' words echoed loudly: "Whoever wants to be my disciple must deny themselves and take up their cross daily and follow me" (Luke 9:23). I discovered that revival is not one dramatic decision but a daily posture of surrender. Not a spark—but a steady flame.

Looking back, I could see how surrender carried me through Austin's miracles, and how surrender would carry me again through deeper valleys ahead. Revival deepened through every season—through the joy of answered prayer and the anguish of unimaginable loss.

I had once believed revival depended on what God gave. But over time, I learned revival was rooted in trusting Him no matter what He allowed or withheld. It grew not because life became easier, but because God proved faithful in every circumstance.

True revival is not an emotional spark, a powerful service, or a moment of tragedy that draws crowds to prayer. Those things may ignite revival—but only surrender sustains it. Revival lasts when God's people remain anchored in His Word, committed to prayer, strengthened by community, and willing to lay everything at His feet.

God had already begun this work in our home. The question now was not if revival had begun—but whether we would remain faithful long after the emotion faded.

Because revival that lasts is revival rooted deeply in Christ alone.

Chapter 8

THE COST
OF REVIVAL

Revival comes when we are willing to
lay down comfort, plans, and even our lives

When I prayed over my son's football locker, "God, whatever it takes to bring him back to You," I had no idea what it would cost. I never imagined it would mean a broken femur, blood clots, or aneurysms. I never pictured nights in the PICU, tears in parking lots, or hearing my son cry out in pain with no answers. But revival always costs something.

For Austin, the cost was physical suffering—painful steps, months of needles, and the interruption of his teenage life. For me, the cost was surrender—letting go of control, even when it felt like it was killing me inside. I learned that revival is never cheap, and the work God does inside us often begins with breaking what we hoped to keep whole.

Jesus never promised ease. He promised the cross.

He said, "Whoever wants to be my disciple must deny themselves and take up their cross daily and follow me. For whoever wants to save their life will lose it, but whoever loses their life for me will save it." (Matthew 16:24–25)

Those words began to take on a new meaning for me. Revival comes when we are willing to lay down our comfort, our plans, and even our lives if necessary.

As I wrestled with this truth, I began to understand that revival has never been cheap. From the earliest days of the church, revival was bought with blood. Stephen, the first Christian martyr, preached boldly before the Sanhedrin. His words cut deeply, and the crowd stoned him. His death looked like defeat, but it became a spark—the believers scattered and carried the gospel farther than it had ever gone before. What seemed like an end was actually a beginning.

James, the brother of John, was put to death by the sword at Herod's command. Peter was imprisoned. Paul was beaten, shipwrecked, and ultimately executed. These men were not inconvenienced; they were crushed. Yet the church grew.

The writer of Hebrews remembered many like them:
"They were stoned; they were sawed in two; they were put to death by the sword. They went about... destitute, persecuted and mistreated—the world was not worthy of them." (Hebrews 11:37–38)

Revival has always demanded that someone lay down their life—whether through literal death or daily surrender.

If revival is going to last in our homes, in our churches, or in our nation, we must accept that it will cost us too. It may cost us comfort when God calls us out of complacency. It may cost us reputation when we choose truth over popularity. It may even cost us relationships when obedience leads to division.

Paul didn't soften this truth:
"Everyone who wants to live a godly life in Christ Jesus will be persecuted." (2 Timothy 3:12)

That isn't a possibility; it's a promise.

This is what I call "convenient Christianity". Convenient Christianity follows Jesus only when it's easy. We worship when the service fits our schedule. We serve when it doesn't cost us. We give only if there's extra. We pray only when crisis strikes. It's faith on our terms—until it threatens comfort. I'm just as guilty of the next person for falling in this trap set meticulously by Satan.

But convenient Christianity cannot sustain revival. It collapses under pressure. True revival is sustained by conviction—by believers who decide Jesus is worth more than their comfort.

The cross is not only where Christ died—it's where we die daily. Revival that costs nothing will never last. But revival that costs everything can never be taken from us, because it is rooted in the One who paid the ultimate price.

Hebrews 12:2 reminds us:
"For the joy set before him he endured the cross, scorning its shame..."

If we are to see revival that truly lasts—in our children, churches, or nation—it will be because we embraced the cost and kept our eyes on Jesus.

Revival is never cheap—but it is always worth it.

Chapter 9

FAITH THAT STANDS WHEN HEADLINES CHANGE

> "No weapon that is formed against you shall prosper." (Isaiah 54:17)

Revival will always cost us something. For the early church, it cost blood. For many bold believers today, it costs their reputations, their comfort, and at times even their lives. For my family, the cost has been years of physical suffering, emotional scars, great loss, and layers of surrender. Yet through it all, God has remained faithful.

Looking back, I see how God wove our story together with strands of mercy and pain. We faced the unexpected death of my niece in 2000. Then came Austin's injury—his femur broken, clots, an aneurysm in 2007, and three miracles that spared his life. At the time, I believed this would be the greatest trial of my motherhood.

I was wrong. It was just the beginning.

Years later, in April 2013, I was in a four-wheeler accident. The handlebar impaled my leg, missing my femoral artery by less than half a centimeter. I was in an isolated dirt pit, all alone, yet God was already there. Doctors later said it was a miracle I survived. That wreck awakened me to how fragile life is—and how much bigger the storms ahead would be.

Five months later, the storm arrived with my youngest son Bryant's, cancer diagnosis at only 17 years old.

His cancer journey began in the same hospital where Austin had been born and where his life had been spared. For 25 months we prayed, we fought, and we hoped. And then—my sweet boy passed away at age 19 the morning after Thanksgiving in 2016.

The same halls that had held life also held grief.

Several years after my son's death, I faced knee surgery on the same injured leg from my four-wheeler accident. Imaging showed a mass—likely scar tissue or a bone spur. The surgeon assured me he could remove it easily during the procedure.

The night before I was scheduled for surgery, everything was unexpectedly moved from an outpatient facility to the hospital operating room and bumped to the first case of the day.

When the surgeon attempted to remove the massive bone spur that had grown out of the hole punched into my femur during the accident, my femoral artery was sliced completely apart. Death was minutes away.

But because the surgery had been moved to the hospital, a cardiac-thoracic surgeon was performing a surgery just a few doors down and was able to repair my artery immediately. My life was spared—again.

Permanent damage to my artery and leg remain, but grace has been much greater. God intervened!

The promise stood firm:
"In all these things we are more than conquerors through Him who loved us." (Romans 8:37)

Austin's suffering and healing, my wreck and rescue, and Bryant's passing became chapters of refining fire. Each one strengthened my faith and prepared me for what would come next.

And then, years later—God brought Austin full circle.

Months before writing this book, he shared that he had been under conviction. He realized that although he prayed to receive Christ as a child, he hadn't truly understood or meant it. He later chose to be baptized again—this time as a grown man - a son, husband, and father, with full conviction. At a public baptism service, he went under the water and rose again—testifying to the grace that had pursued him all his life.

The boy whose leg was broken, whose life was spared three times, whose vow in the PICU was delayed by my bitterness—now walked boldly in the calling I once prayed over his football locker.

Austin's story, Bryant's story, and mine all declare this:
God is faithful.
Even when the fire fades.
Even when we stumble.
Even when the headlines move on.

The call is the same for every believer—will we build revival on fleeting emotion, or on faith that stands firm?

Galatians 6:9 reminds us:
"Let us not become weary in doing good, for at the proper time we will reap a harvest if we do not give up."

That is the call—to stand when news cycles shift, to worship when feelings fade, and to pray, "God, whatever it takes for revival to last—do it."

Because faith that endures is faith that revives.
And revival that lasts is rooted in Christ alone.

Chapter 10

WHEN THE ENEMY STRIKES BACK

When revival begins to stir, the enemy doesn't retreat.

When revival begins to stir, the enemy does not sit quietly. He prowls, schemes, and strikes. His mission remains the same: to steal, kill, and destroy (John 10:10). When he cannot silence believers through suffering, he will attempt to crush them through tragedy.

August 1, 2025 brought another blow.

Austin's father had been living with serious, ongoing health issues that brought a slow decline and uncertainty to his life. Still, the end came without warning.

That afternoon, Austin's dad ran a stop sign on a familiar road and collided with an eighteen-wheeler. Austin arrived at the scene within minutes. He didn't see his father's body, but he recognized the mangled vehicle. The grief was immediate.

Questions followed. Why would he run a stop sign he knew well? Troopers suspected a medical emergency. An autopsy was originally ordered but never performed, leaving questions unanswered.

Yet even here, God gave mercy.

Three days later, Austin returned to the crash site and found his father's phone. Despite heavy rain, the phone still worked. When Austin called the number, it rang—and the call history showed that just moments before impact, his father had dialed 911. He knew something was wrong and called for help.

The discovery brought comfort—suggesting he likely passed before the collision, spared from the impact and the flames. Because his body remained whole, Austin was able to have closure with an open casket.

We believed God showed mercy—sparing him and those who loved him from prolonged suffering. We knew the toll of long illness; we had watched Bryant endure 25 hard months.

Scripture warns us:
"Your enemy the devil prowls around like a roaring lion looking for someone to devour." (1 Peter 5:8–9)

The enemy has always attempted to silence God's people—through violence, intimidation, division, and despair. Yet every time, God turns evil for good.

Genesis 50:20 reminds us:
"You intended to harm me, but God intended it for good…"

Even in the shock of sudden loss, God's mercy threaded through.
Faith remained.
And revival continued.

Because revival doesn't silence attacks—it attracts them. But revival that lasts is not destroyed by tragedy; it is refined through it.

The enemy may roar, but God's faithfulness roars louder.
He continues to answer the prayer:
"God, whatever it takes."

Even when the cost is high.
Even when the pain is deep.
He remains faithful.

WHATEVER IT TAKES FOR REVIVAL TO LAST

When I prayed over Austin's football locker, whispering, "God, whatever it takes to bring him back to You," I never imagined the weight of those words.

I didn't know it would mean a broken femur, blood clots, and aneurysms.
I didn't know it would mean sleepless nights in the NICU, hard conversations, and tears in parking lots.

I didn't know it would mean a four-wheeler wreck, a severed femoral artery, surgeries, scars, or permanent damage.

I didn't know it would mean the deaths of my parents within months of each other—or the unthinkable heartbreak of watching my youngest son, Bryant, endure a 25-month battle with cancer and take his final breath in the same hospital where Austin's life had been spared.

I didn't know it would mean watching Austin lose his father suddenly… or standing at the edge of that wreckage.

But God knew.

And He knew every detail would become a testimony of His sustaining grace.

Through it all, God answered that dangerous prayer.
Austin's faith was tested, refined, and restored.
From a locker-room whisper to a public baptism as a grown man, God completed the work He began.

Bryant's story continues too—through the lives he touched, through the testimony we share, and through every grieving parent who finds comfort in his courage. What the enemy intended for destruction, God has used to bring hope.

Now I can see that my prayer was never just about Austin—or even about my family.
It was about revival.
Revival in homes.
Revival in churches.
Revival in a nation longing for truth.

A revival not rooted in emotion or crisis, but in faith that endures.

The enemy has not stopped striking.
But he has not won.

Because Scripture promises:
"Greater is He that is in you than he that is in the world." (1 John 4:4)
"They overcame by the blood of the Lamb and the word of their testimony." (Revelation 12:11)
"He who began a good work in you will carry it on to completion..." (Philippians 1:6)

That is the anchor.
That is the hope.
That is what makes revival last.

Because when God's people dare to pray,
"Whatever it takes,"
—and mean it—
revival begins...
and by His power, it will remain.

REFERENCE LIST

Romans 8:28

And we know that in all things God works for the good of those who love him, who have been called according to his purpose.

John 16:33

"I have told you these things, so that in me you may have peace. In this world you will have trouble. But take heart! I have overcome the world."

Genesis 50:20

You intended to harm me, but God intended it for good to accomplish what is now being done, the saving of many lives.

Job 13:15

Though he slay me, yet will I hope in him; I will surely defend my ways to his face.

Hebrews 12:6

because the Lord disciplines the one he loves, and he chastens everyone he accepts as his son.

Hebrews 12:15

See to it that no one falls short of the grace of God and that no bitter root grows up to cause trouble and defile many.

1 Peter 4:12–13

Dear friends, do not be surprised at the fiery ordeal that has come on you to test you, as though something strange were happening to you. But rejoice inasmuch as you participate in the sufferings of Christ, so that you may be overjoyed when his glory is revealed.

Luke 8:13

Those on the rocky ground are the ones who receive the word with joy when they hear it, but they have no root. They believe for a while, but in the time of testing they fall away.

Hebrews 12:1–2

Therefore, since we are surrounded by such a great cloud of witnesses, let us throw off everything that hinders and the sin that so easily entangles. And let us run with perseverance the race marked out for us, fixing our eyes on Jesus, the pioneer and perfecter of faith. For the joy set before him he endured the cross, scorning its shame, and sat down at the right hand of the throne of God.

Matthew 24:35

Heaven and earth will pass away, but my words will never pass away.

1 Thessalonians 5:17

pray continually,

Acts 2:42

They devoted themselves to the apostles' teaching and to fellowship, to the breaking of bread and to prayer.

Luke 9:23

Then he said to them all: "Whoever wants to be my disciple must deny themselves and take up their cross daily and follow me."

John 15:4–5

Remain in me, as I also remain in you. No branch can bear fruit by itself; it must remain in the vine. Neither can you bear fruit unless you remain in me. I am the vine; you are the branches. If you remain in me and I in you, you will bear much fruit; apart from me you can do nothing.

Matthew 16:24–25

Then Jesus said to his disciples, "Whoever wants to be my disciple must deny themselves and take up their cross and follow me. For whoever wants to save their life will lose it, but whoever loses their life for me will find it."

Acts 7:60

Then he fell on his knees and cried out, "Lord, do not hold this sin against them." When he had said this, he fell asleep.

Acts 12:1–5

It was about this time that King Herod arrested some who belonged to the church, intending to persecute them. He had James, the brother of John, put to death with the sword. When he saw that this met with approval among the Jews, he proceeded to seize Peter also. This happened during the Festival of Unleavened Bread. After arresting him, he put him in prison, handing him over to be guarded by four squads of four soldiers each. Herod intended to bring him out for public trial after the Passover. So Peter was kept in prison, but the church was earnestly praying to God for him.

Hebrews 11:37–38

They were put to death by stoning; they were sawed in two; they were killed by the sword. They went about in sheepskins and goatskins, destitute, persecuted and mistreated— the world was not worthy of them. They wandered in deserts and mountains, living in caves and in holes in the ground.

2 Timothy 3:12

In fact, everyone who wants to live a godly life in Christ Jesus will be persecuted,

Hebrews 12:2

fixing our eyes on Jesus, the pioneer and perfecter of faith. For the joy set before him he endured the cross, scorning its shame, and sat down at the right hand of the throne of God.

Isaiah 54:17

no weapon forged against you will prevail, and you will refute every tongue that accuses you. This is the heritage of the servants of the Lord, and this is their vindication from me," declares the Lord.

Romans 8:37

No, in all these things we are more than conquerors through him who loved us.

Galatians 6:9

Let us not become weary in doing good, for at the proper time we will reap a harvest if we do not give up.

REVIVAL BEGINS
WITH SALVATION

If you long for genuine revival—in your heart, home, or nation—it must begin with a personal relationship with Jesus Christ. Revival doesn't start with packed churches or emotional moments; it starts with one life surrendered to Him.

The Bible makes it clear
- *We all need a Savior.*

"For all have sinned and fall short of the glory of God." (Romans 3:23 NIV)

- *Sin separates us from God.*

"For the wages of sin are death, but the gift of God is eternal life in Christ Jesus our Lord." (Romans 6:23 NIV)

- *God provided the way.*

"But God demonstrates his own love for us in this: While we were still sinners, Christ died for us." (Romans 5:8 NIV)

- *Salvation is a gift, received by faith.*

"If you declare with your mouth, 'Jesus is Lord,' and believe in your heart that God raised him from the dead, you will be saved." (Romans 10:9 NIV)

- You can call on Him right now.

"Everyone who calls on the name of the Lord will be saved." (Romans 10:13)

A Simple Prayer of Salvation

"Lord Jesus, I know that I am a sinner and I need Your forgiveness. I believe that You died on the cross for my sins and arose again. Today, I turn from my sin and invite You into my heart and life. I trust You as my Savior and choose to follow You as Lord. In Jesus' name. Amen."

Next Steps in Revival

If you just prayed that prayer and meant it, you are now a child of God! Revival begins in you today.

- Read God's Word Daily - start with the Gospel of John.
- Pray Daily - talk to God as your Father.
- Find a Bible-believing church - you need community to grow strong.
- Be Baptized - declare your faith publicly as the early church did.
- Share your Story - revival spreads when testimonies are told.

Revival that lasts is not about feelings but daily surrender. Jesus said, "Whoever wants to be my disciple must deny themselves and take up their cross daily and follow me." (Luke 9:23 NIV)

Revival That Lasts

Revival begins when one sinner repents and turns to Christ, and it continues as believers walk daily with Him. If you've just prayed to receive Christ, you are now part of something eternal—something no news cycle, tragedy, or trial can ever take away.

Welcome to the family of God.
Revival has begun in you.

DISCUSSION & REFLECTION GUIDE

Introduction: The Dangerous Prayer

Key Scripture

"Whoever wants to be my disciple must deny themselves and take up their cross daily and follow me."
(Luke 9:23, NIV)

Reflection Thought

Revival begins with surrender. Dangerous prayers ask God to move, not on our terms, but on His—even if it means pain, loss, or waiting.

Questions for Reflection

- What areas of my life have I been reluctant to surrender to God?

- How could praying "whatever it takes" deepen my faith?

Prayer

Lord, give me courage to surrender everything to You.
Teach me to trust that Your ways are higher than mine.

Chapter 1 - The Prayer Over the Locker

Key Scripture

"Trust in the Lord with all your heart and lean not on your own
understanding; in all your ways submit to him,
and he will make your paths straight."
(Proverbs 3:5–6, NIV)

Reflection Thought

A mother's prayer at a locker became the seed of revival.
True surrender releases our grip and trusts God
with what we hold most dear.

Questions for Reflection

- Who do I need to surrender to God in prayer today?

- What might trusting God "with all my heart" look like in my
daily life?

Prayer

Father, I release my loved ones into Your care.
Lead them back to You in Your perfect way and timing.

Chapter 2- The Test Begins

Key Scripture

"And we know that in all things God works for the good of those who love him, who have been called according to his purpose." (Romans 8:28, NIV)

Reflection Thought

When life falls apart, God is still writing a story of redemption. What feels like harm, He can use for good.

Questions for Reflection

- Where have I seen God bring good out of painful circumstances?

- How can I hold on to His promises when fear threatens my faith?

Prayer

Lord, remind me that nothing is wasted in Your hands. Strengthen my faith when life feels out of control. Amen.

Chapter 3 - In The Valley of Decision

Key Scripture

"Consider it pure joy, my brothers and sisters, whenever you face trials of many kinds, because you know that the testing of your faith produces perseverance." (James 1:2–3, NIV)

Reflection Thought

Even in the valley, God's hand is at work. Our trials refine us, teaching us to rely on Him and producing a deeper perseverance.

Questions for Reflection

• How have my valleys produced perseverance in my life?

• Where do I need to trust God's hand even when I can't see the outcome?

Prayer

God, give me eyes to see Your hand in my trials. Shape me through them into who You are calling me to be. Amen.

Chapter 4 - Held In His Hands

Key Scripture
"Though he slay me, yet will I hope in him."
(Job 13:15, NIV)

Reflection Thought
God's miracles often come in unexpected ways—
sometimes through healing, sometimes
through the quiet gift of sustaining faith.

Questions for Reflection
- Where has God shown up miraculously in my life?

- Do I trust Him to be faithful even if His answer
isn't what I expected?

Prayer
Lord, help me see Your miracles, big and small, and give me the
faith to trust You no matter the outcome. Amen.

Chapter 5 - Where I Fell Short

Key Scripture

"See to it that no one falls short of the grace of God
and that no bitter root grows up to cause trouble
and defile many." (Hebrews 12:15, NIV)

Reflection Thought

Bitterness is the enemy of revival. When we focus
on people's failures instead of God's faithfulness,
our hearts harden, and we stumble.

Questions for Reflection

- Where am I holding on to bitterness instead
of surrendering to God?

- How can I root my faith in Christ rather than
in people's actions?

Prayer

Father, forgive me where I've allowed bitterness to take root. Help
me fix my eyes on Your faithfulness instead. Amen.

Chapter 6 - When The Fire Fades

Key Scripture

"Therefore, since we are surrounded by such a great cloud of witnesses, let us throw off everything that hinders and the sin that so easily entangles. And let us run with perseverance the race marked out for us, fixing our eyes on Jesus."
(Hebrews 12:1–2, NIV)

Reflection Thought

Revival is not sustained by emotion but by perseverance. Just as faith must be lived daily,
revival must be nurtured daily.

Questions for Reflection

• Where has my fire for God faded?

• What daily practices help me fix my eyes on Jesus?

Prayer

Lord, rekindle my fire for You. Help me
in run the race with endurance and faithfulness.

Chapter 7 - Revival That Last

Key Scripture

"Wake up, sleeper, rise from the dead, and Christ will shine on you." (Ephesians 5:14, NIV)

Reflection Thought

True revival is not an emotional spark but a lasting transformation. It is sustained through the Word, prayer, community, and surrender.

Questions for Reflection

- Which of these four—Word, prayer, community, surrender—do I need to strengthen in my life?

- What does "revival that lasts" look like for me personally?

Prayer

Lord, awaken my heart to You again. Let my life be rooted in Your truth and strengthened by Your Spirit.

Chapter 8 - The Cost of Revival

Key Scripture

"Everyone who wants to live a godly life in Christ Jesus will be persecuted." (2 Timothy 3:12, NIV)

Reflection Thought

Revival has always cost something. It requires surrender, conviction, and faith that stands even in persecution.

Questions for Reflection

- What cost am I willing to pay for Christ?

- Where has my faith been challenged, and how did I respond?

Prayer

Jesus, give me courage to stand for You, no matter the cost. Amen.

Chapter 9 - Faith That Stands When The Headlines Change

Key Scripture

"Let us not become weary in doing good, for at the proper time we will reap a harvest if we do not give up." (Galatians 6:9, NIV)

Reflection Thought

Headlines fade, but faith endures. The test of revival is whether it still stands when the news cycle moves on.

Questions for Reflection

- Am I building my faith on headlines and emotion, or on Christ alone?

- How can I live faithfully when the world is distracted or divided?

Prayer

Lord, give me perseverance when the spotlight fades. Help me live faithfully, rooted in You.

Chapter 9 - When The Enemy Strikes Back

Key Scripture

"Be alert and of sober mind. Your enemy the devil prowls around like a roaring lion looking for someone to devour. Resist him, standing firm in the faith."
(1 Peter 5:8–9, NIV)

Reflection Thought

Revival draws attack. But what Satan means for evil, God redeems for His glory.

Questions for Reflection

- Where have I felt the enemy's attacks in my own life?

- How can I stand firm in God's promises during spiritual battles?

Prayer

God, make me strong to resist the enemy.
Let my life bring glory to You, even in the battle. Amen.

Conclusion – Whatever It Takes For Revival To Last

Key Scripture

"Being confident of this, that he who began a good work in you will carry it on to completion until the day of Christ Jesus."
(Philippians 1:6, NIV)

Reflection Thought

Revival that lasts is not built on emotion but on God's faithfulness. The same God who began the work will finish it.

Questions for Reflection

- Where have I seen God's faithfulness carry me through?

- What does "whatever it takes" look like in my own walk with Christ?

Prayer

Lord, complete the work You have begun in me.
Let my life bear fruit for Your glory until the very end. Amen.

REVIEW

I couldn't put it down – highly recommend

Easy to read!

A powerful message

Would you please consider leaving a review of my book on Amazon?

It's super easy and helps
promote my books.
Go to Amazon and search for my
book by title or my name.
Once you're on the book's page, scroll
down until you see
"Write a customer review".
Click it, choose your star rating,
add a short comment,
and then submit.
That's it - quick and easy!

WITH MY FATHER'S HANDS
PUBLISHING

30-Day Companion Devotional

for

God, Whatever It Takes for Revival To Last

This 30-day devotional was born from a prayer over a football locker and the journey that followed: through miracles, loss, and healing, God taught author, Janet Little Cooper, that revival is not a moment—it's a way of life. The goal is for these daily reflections to lead you closer to Him, stirring a personal awakening that doesn't fade when the emotions do.

Available on

amazon

ORDER your Copy TODAY!

Cover is sold in Color

Each day offers a story from Cooper's life, a passage from Scripture, and time to reflect, pray, and apply what God is teaching. You don't need perfect faith—just a willing heart. Because God can take one small act of surrender and use it to spark something eternal.

THE BEFORE AND AFTER OF LOSS

A Faithful-Filled Guide To Walking Through Illness, Death, and Grief

About the Book

The Before and After of Loss is a powerful story of a mother's faith through heartbreak. When Janet's 19-year-old son, Bryant, battled cancer, God met her in the pain and carried her through grief into hope. With raw honesty and gentle encouragement, this book offers comfort and purpose to anyone walking through loss or supporting someone who is.

Author: Janet Little Cooper
Publisher: With My Father's Hands Publishing
Email: myfathershands@gmail.com:

Retail Price: $18.99
Available on Audible,
Amazon Kindle and Paperback
*Cover of actual book is in color

Available on Amazon

Endorsements

"Love that flows from the heart of a grieving mother is deep. Janet Little Cooper knows the pain and the healing process of loss. Her book will encourage you and help you comfort others. Read it to learn of love that never fails."

— Pastor Ted Traylor, Olive Baptist Church, Pensacola, FL

While we all hope to be spared the loss of a child, one situation most of us are likely to face is that of comforting a friend or acquaintance who has lost theirs. In her newest release, "The Before and After of Loss", Janet Little Cooper not only details her journey, but gives practical advice on how we can really help. This is an important book."

— Andy Andrews, New York Times bestselling author of The Traveler's Gift and The Noticer

"If my people, who are
called by my name,
will humble themselves
and pray and seek my face
and turn from their
wicked ways, then I will
hear from heaven,
and I will forgive their sin
and will heal their land."
2 Chronicles 7:14

The Manger Counts Down To Christmas

The manger whispers, "Come and see— A baby's born for you and me!" Each day a friend joins in to cheer "The Savior of the world is here!" A cow, a star, a donkey too, All share the joy so bright and true.

By Janet Little Cooper

FULL COLOR
HARDBACK
8.5 x 11 inches

Come count the days, one by one, To the birth of God's own Son—The greatest gift, so small and mild, God's love was born in Heaven's child.

Day 7—
It's The
Innkeeper

Knock, knock!

"No room," said the innkeeper.

But he shared his stable

— and that's where I live!

Available On
amazon

Day 26—
The
Holy Night!

Also, Includes the full Christmas Story as told in the International Children's Bible®, written in words even little hearts can understand.

"For I will pour out water to quench your thirst and to irrigate your parched fields. And I will pour out my Spirit on your descendants, and my blessing on your children."
Isaiah 44:3 (NLT)

What God starts, He finishes.
What breaks your heart, He redeems.
And what you surrender, He uses for His glory.

www.ingramcontent.com/pod-product-compliance
Lightning Source LLC
Chambersburg PA
CBHW051647120626
46551CB00015B/2250